FRESHWATER

BOOKS BY VIRGINIA WOOLF

The Voyage Out, 1915

Night and Day, 1919

Kew Gardens, 1919

Monday or Tuesday, 1921

Jacob's Room, 1922

The Common Reader: First Series, 1925

Mrs. Dalloway, 1925

To the Lighthouse, 1927

Orlando, 1928

A Room of One's Own, 1929

The Waves, 1931

Letter to a Young Poet, 1932

The Second Common Reader, 1932

Flush, 1933

The Years, 1937

Three Guineas, 1938

Roger Fry: A Biography, 1940

Between the Acts, 1941

The Death of the Moth and Other Essays, 1942

A Haunted House and Other Short Stories, 1944

The Moment and Other Essays, 1947

The Captain's Death Bed and Other Essays, 1950

A Writer's Diary, 1954

Virginia Woolf and Lytton Strachey: Letters, 1956

Granite and Rainbow, 1958

Contemporary Writers, 1965

Collected Essays (*4 vols.*), 1967

Mrs. Dalloway's Party, 1973

The Letters of Virginia Woolf. Vol. I: 1888–1912, 1975

Freshwater, 1976

Angelica Garnett in the role of Ellen Terry

Photograph by Vanessa Bell. © *1976 by Angelica Garnett.*

VIRGINIA WOOLF

FRESHWATER

· A COMEDY ·

Edited and with a Preface
by Lucio P. Ruotolo

Illustrated by Loretta Trezzo

Harcourt Brace Jovanovich · New York and London

Printed in the United States of America

Library of Congress Cataloging in Publication Data

Woolf, Virginia Stephen, 1882–1941.
Freshwater : a comedy.
I. Title.
PR6045.072F7   1976   822'.9'12   76-1902
ISBN 0-15-133487-0

First edition

B C D E

EDITOR'S PREFACE

The 1935 performance of *Freshwater*, a play Virginia Woolf had written twelve years earlier and then completely revised for this occasion, was one of a number of theatrical evenings that had characterized "Bloomsbury" parties since the early 1920s. These entertainments ranged from a production of Milton's *Comus* to variety-show skits that could be, in Virginia's own words, "sublimely obscene." Among the earlier comedies, David Garnett recalls in his autobiography, was a play entitled *Don't Be Frightened, or Pippington Park*, inspired by the newspaper report of a wealthy gentleman who had molested a young woman in the park. Vanessa Bell played the victim, and the last act featured a *pas de deux* by Lydia Lopokova and Maynard Keynes. One play written by Quentin Bell presented his home at Charleston as an archeological ruin of the distant future, visited by tourists. Bell also remembers a comic drama in rhymed couplets called *The Last Days of Old Pompeii*. These performances were given at a number of different residences.

Freshwater appears to be one of a series of later plays staged in the mid-1930s in Vanessa Bell's London studio at 8 Fitzroy Street. Among them was a shadow play about John the Baptist, which featured a protruding severed head made by Duncan Grant out of cardboard and oozing red gelatin.

Vanessa's studio was L-shaped, with the spectators at these occasions seated in the long part of the L and a curtained stage extending from the short part. On the evening of 18 January 1935, there was evidently a full house of about eighty guests, who had come at the special invitation of "Mrs. Clive Bell and Mrs. Leonard Woolf" to attend *"Freshwater*, A Comedy." The event also celebrated Angelica Bell's recent birthday.

The audience was in a party mood from the very outset and the play, which began at 9:30, was performed in an atmosphere of noise and levity. Clive Bell's booming voice and laughter in particular were heard throughout the performance. Since the stage lighting was dim it was not always possible to see, let alone to hear, what was going on. But Virginia's diary entry of the following day records her own appreciation of this "unbuttoned laughing evening." The production, however marred, as well as the writing of *Freshwater*, clearly gave her pleasure.

The performance room was connected by a wooden passageway, roofed in corrugated iron, to Duncan Grant's adjoining studio. After the final curtain, the assembly of guests and players moved, as was the custom, down the rumbling hallway for a party in Duncan's quarters. The party after *Freshwater* was predictably long and festive.

While these Bloomsbury plays were done in a jolly ambience, their preparation usually involved a great deal of time and hard work for both writers and players. This was especially so in the case of *Freshwater*. Rehearsals for the play continued throughout the preceding summer, and even a casual study of the text shows how fully Virginia had researched the subject of her great-aunt Julia Margaret Cameron. The notes to *Freshwater* intend to give only a few examples of the characteristic thoroughness with which she approached even such less serious projects.

The two manuscripts of the play, published here for the first time, were discovered by Olivier Bell in 1969, a few weeks after Leonard Woolf's death. Leonard Woolf had known of their existence among the vast accumulation of papers in Monk's House, but he could not locate them when Quentin Bell first asked him about Virginia's unpublished play.

The problem of identifying these two texts is complicated by the fact that none of the surviving spectators and players interviewed could be certain which version was performed in 1935. Quentin Bell is among a number of people who received invitations but could not attend. Having missed the actual performance staged in his mother's studio, he was forced in preparing the first drafts of his aunt's biography to reconstruct the play from the recollection of rehearsals he had attended at Charleston. Quentin Bell's notes offer the best proof for dating at least one of the two versions, since he wrote them before his wife found the manuscripts and they record two incidents which occur only in the text beginning "Sit still, Charles." The two incidents are Tennyson's poem on a young woman drowned and, more crucially, the scene on the beach between Ellen Terry and John Craig.

A handwritten transcription by Vanessa of her role as Mrs. Cameron, which includes a cast list, offers further proof. With one important exception (see pages 75–76) she has written down the part as we find it in the "Sit still, Charles" version.

Angelica Garnett recently discovered another cast list, this one in Virginia's hand, which offers a somewhat different and evidently more accurate *Dramatis Personae* (see page 3). While differing cast lists might suggest another performance of the revised play, I find no evidence that more than one ever took place.

Vanessa Bell's notes are housed, along with the two versions of *Freshwater*, at the University of Sussex Library, Brighton.

Although the "unrevised" first version of *Freshwater*, included here in the Appendix, is somewhat harder to date, an examination of typescript and of internal references supports Quentin Bell's assertion that it was written in 1923.

As early as 1919, Virginia states her intention to write a comedy about Julia Cameron. In her diary entry for 8 July 1923, she describes herself working vigorously on "Freshwater, A Comedy," a welcome diversion in her struggle with "The Hours" (*Mrs. Dalloway*). She expects to complete the play on the next day. Six weeks later in a letter to Vanessa, Virginia expresses concern that the play is not yet finished and invites her sister and Duncan Grant to hear it read "as soon as possible." The urgency suggests a deadline and is clarified by her letter to Desmond MacCarthy, probably written in October of that same year, asking if he would consider stage-managing the play for a Christmas production. He agreed to direct *Freshwater*; Virginia, however, deeply involved in the writing of her novel, disappointed a number of people by deciding to abandon the production. "I could write something much better," she informs Vanessa in the late fall of 1923, "if I gave up a little more time to it: and I foresee that the whole affair will be much more of an undertaking than I thought." She was to find time to improve her play a decade later.

Readers should be aware that the two manuscripts of

the play were typed rapidly and for oral presentation. They are often without punctuation and filled with spelling and typographical errors. Obviously misspelled words have been corrected and punctuation added where the sense of the passage requires it, more extensively in inaccurately quoted verses. Where Virginia's handwritten additions and emendations are only partly legible, I have omitted them entirely. Otherwise, I have tried to reproduce the texts as they appear in manuscript.

My special thanks to Olivier and Quentin Bell, to Angelica Garnett and to Nigel Nicolson, all of whom supplied valuable information for preparing this edition.

My thanks also to Anita Ventura Mozley, Curator of Photography at the Stanford University Museum of Art, for first pointing out to me how much of *Freshwater* is built upon fact, not fiction, and to John Graham, Duncan Grant, John Lehmann, Tom Lewis, Trekkie and Ian Parsons, Ann Jellicoe, Pat Rosenbaum, Susan Squier, Lola Szladits, and Joanne Trautmann for offering their time and help.

Finally, I thankfully acknowledge The University of Sussex Library and the Henry W. and Albert A. Berg Collection of The New York Public Library, Astor, Lenox and Tilden Foundations, for permission to quote from unpublished Virginia Woolf letters.

LUCIO P. RUOTOLO

Monk's House
September 1975

FRESHWATER

Dramatis Personae.

Julia Margaret Cameron ————— Vanessa Bell.
Charles Hay Cameron, her
         husband, ——— Leonard Woolf.
George Frederick Watts ——— Duncan Grant.
      R.A.
Ellen Terry ——————— Angelica Bell.
    wife of G. F. Watts
Alfred Tennyson   Adrian Stephen
    poet laureate.
Mary Magdalen —   Ann Stephen.
the maid.
John Lieutenant John Craig   Julian Bell.
       R.N.
Queen Victoria ——— Eve Younger.
The Porpoise ———— Judith Stephen.
The Marmoset.   Mitzi.

Virginia Woolf's casting for *Freshwater*

ACT I

ACT I

A studio. MRS. CAMERON *washing* MR. CAMERON's *head.*
ELLEN TERRY *on the model's throne posing to* WATTS *for*
Modesty at the feet of Mammon.

MRS. C.

> Sit still, Charles! Sit still! Soap in your eyes? Non-
> sense. Water down your back? Tush! Surely you can
> put up with a little discomfort in the cause of art!

MR. C.

> The sixth time in eight months! The sixth time in
> eight months! Whenever we start for India Julia
> washes my head. And yet we never do start for India.
> I sometimes think we never shall start for India.

MRS. C.

> Nonsense, Charles. Control yourself, Charles. Remem-
> ber what Alfred Tennyson said of you: A philosopher
> with his beard dipped in moonlight. A chimney-sweep
> with his beard dipped in soot.

MR. C.

> Ah, if we could but go to India. There is no washing
> in India. There beards are white, for the moon for
> ever shines, on youth, on truth, in India. And here we
> dally, frittering away our miserable lives in the
> withered grasp of—

[MRS. C. *washes vigorously.*]

WATTS [*looking round*]
Courage, my old friend. Courage. The Utmost for the Highest, Cameron. Always remember that. [*to* ELLEN] Don't move, Ellen. Keep yourself perfectly still. I am struggling with the great toe of Mammon. I have been struggling for six months. It is still out of drawing. But I say to myself, The Utmost for the Highest. Keep perfectly still.

[*Enter* TENNYSON.]

TENN.
The son of man has nowhere to lay his head!

MR. C.
Washing day at Farringford too, Alfred?

TENN.
Twenty earnest youths from Clerkenwell are in the shrubbery; six American professors are in the summer house; the bathroom is occupied by the Ladies Poetry Circle from Ohio. The son of man has nowhere to lay his head.

MR. C.
Loose your mind from the affairs of the present. Seek truth where truth lies hidden. Follow the everlasting will o' the wisp. Oh don't tug my beard! [MRS. C. *releases him.*] Heaven be praised! At two thirty we start for India. [MR. C. *walks away to the window.*]

TENN.
Upon my word! You don't say you're really going?

8

MRS. C. [*wringing out her sponge*]

Yes, Alfred. At two thirty we start for India—that's to say if the coffins have come. [MRS. C. *gives the sponge to* MARY.] Take my sponge, girl; now go and see if the coffins have come.

MARY

If the coffins have come! Why, it's the Earl of Dudley who's come. He's waiting for me in the kitchen. He's not much to look at but he's a deal sight better than coffins any day.

MRS. C.

We can't start for India without our coffins. For the eighth time I have ordered the coffins, and for the eighth time the coffins have not come. But without her coffin Julia Cameron will not start for India. Think, Alfred. When we lie dead under the Southern Cross my head will be pillowed upon your immortal poem *In Memoriam*. *Maud* will lie upon my heart. Look—Orion glitters in the southern sky. The scent of tulip-trees is wafted through the open window. The silence is only broken by the sobs of my husband and the occasional howl of a solitary tiger. And then what is this—what infamy do I perceive? An ant, Alfred, a white ant. They are advancing in hordes from the jungle. Alfred, they are devouring *Maud!*

TENN.

God bless my soul! Devouring *Maud?* The white ants! My ewe lamb! That's true. You can't go to India without your coffins. And how am I going to read *Maud* to you when you're in India? Still—what's the time? Twelve fifteen? I've read it in less. Let's begin.

9

I hate the dreadful hollow behind the little wood,
Its lips in the field above are dabbled with
blood-red heath,
The red-ribb'd ledges drip with a silent horror
of blood,
And Echo there, whatever is ask'd her, answers
"Death."

For there in the ghastly pit long since a body was
found,
His who had given me life—O father! O God!—

MRS. C.

That's the very attitude I want! Sit still, Alfred. Don't blink your eyes. Charles, you're sitting on my lens. Get up.

[MRS. C. *fixes her tripod.* TENNYSON *goes on reading* Maud.]

ELLEN [*stretching her arms*]
Oh, Signor, can't I get down? I am so stiff.

WATTS

Stiff, Ellen? Why you've only kept that pose for four hours this morning.

ELLEN

Only four hours! It seems like centuries. Anyhow I'm awfully stiff. And I would so like to go for a bathe. It's a lovely morning. The bees on the thorn. [ELLEN *clambers down off the model's throne and stretches herself.*]

10

WATTS

You have given four hours to the service of art, Ellen, and are already tired. I have given seventy-seven years to the service of art and I am not tired yet.

ELLEN

O Lor'!

WATTS

If you must use that vulgar expression, Ellen, please sound the final *d*.

ELLEN [*standing beside* TENNYSON]

Oh Lord, Lord, Lord!

TENN.

I am not yet a Lord, damsel; but who knows? That may lie on the lap of the Queen. Meanwhile, sit on *my* lap.

[ELLEN *sits on* TENNYSON's *knee.*]

MRS. C.

Another picture! A better picture! Poetry in the person of Alfred Tennyson adoring the Muse.

ELLEN

But I'm Modesty, Mrs. Cameron; Signor said so. I'm Modesty crouching at the feet of Mammon, at least I was ten minutes ago.

MRS. C.

Yes. But now you're the Muse. But the Muse must have wings. [MRS. C. *rummages frantically in a chest.*

11

She flings out various garments on the floor.] Towels, sheets, pyjamas, trousers, dressing gowns, braces— braces but no wings. Trousers but no wings. What a satire upon modern life! Braces but no wings! [MRS. C. *goes to the door and shouts:*] Wings! Wings! Wings! What d'you say, Mary. There are no wings? Then kill the turkey! [MRS. C. *shuffles among the clothes. She exits.*]

TENN. [*to* ELLEN]
You're a very beautiful wench, Ellen!

ELLEN
And you're a very great poet, Mr. Tennyson.

TENN.
Did you ever see a poet's skin? [*He pulls up his sleeve and shows her his arm.*]

ELLEN
Like a crumpled rose leaf!

TENN.
Ah, but you should see me in my bath! I have thighs like alabaster!

ELLEN
I sometimes think, Mr. Tennyson, that you are the most sensible of them all.

TENN. [*kissing her*]
I am sensible to beauty in all its forms. That is my function as Poet Laureate.

ELLEN

Tell me, Mr. Tennyson, have you ever picked primroses in a lane?

TENN.

Scores of times.

ELLEN

And did Lady Tennyson ever jump over your head
on a horse?

TENN.

Emily jump? Emily jump? She has lain on her sofa
for fifty years and I should be surprised, nay I should
be shocked, if she ever got up again.

ELLEN

Then I suppose you were never in love. Nobody ever
jumped over your head and dropped a white rose into
your hand and galloped away?

TENN.

Hallam never galloped. He had a bad seat on horseback. My life has been singularly free from amorous
excitement of the kind you describe. Tell me more.

ELLEN

Well you see, Mr. Tennyson, I was walking in a lane
the other day picking primroses when—

MRS. C. [*re-entering*]
Here's the turkey wings.

13

ELLEN

Oh, Mrs. Cameron, have you killed the turkey? And I was so fond of that bird.

MRS. C.

The turkey is happy, Ellen. The turkey has become part and parcel of my immortal art. Now, Ellen. Mount this chair. Throw your arms out. Look upwards. Alfred, you too—look up!

TENN.

To Nell!

WATTS

I do not altogether approve of the composition of this piece, Julia.

MRS. C.

The Utmost for the Highest, Signor. Now, keep perfectly still. Only for fifteen minutes.

MR. C. [*looking at the marmoset*]
Life is a dream.

TENN.

Rather a wet one, Charles.

MR. C.

All things that have substance seem to me unreal. What are these? [*He picks up the braces.*] Braces. Fetters that bind us to the wheel of life. What are these? [*He picks up the trousers.*] Trousers. Fig leaves that conceal the truth. What is truth? Moonshine. Where does the moon shine for ever? India. Come, my marmoset, let us go to India. Let us go to India, the land of our dreams. [*He walks to the window. A whistle sounds in the garden.*]

ELLEN

I come! I come! [*She jumps down and rushes out of the room.*]

MRS. C.

She's spoilt my picture!

TENN.

My picture too.

MRS. C.

The girl's mad. The girl's gone clean out of her wits. What can she want to go bathing for when she might be sitting to me?

TENN. [*opens* Maud *and begins reading*]
Well:

> Come into the garden, Maud,
>   For the black bat, night, has flown,
> Come into the garden, Maud,
>   I am here at the gate alone—

WATTS

Alfred, tell me. Is your poetry based on fact?

TENN.

Certainly it is. I never describe a daisy without putting it under the microscope first. Listen.

> For her feet have touch'd the meadows
>   And left the daisies rosy.

Why did I say "rosy"? Because it is a fact—

15

MR. C.

I thought I saw something which many people would call a fact pass the window just now. A fact in trousers; a fact in side whiskers; a handsome fact, as facts go. A young man, in fact.

MRS. C.

A young man! Just what I want. A young man with noble thighs, ambrosial locks and eyes of gold. [*She goes to the window and calls out:*] Young man! Young man! I want you to come and sit to me for Sir Isumbras at the Ford. [*She exits. A donkey brays. She comes back into the room.*] That's not a man. That's a donkey. Still, to the true artist, one fact is much the same as another. A fact is a fact; art is art; a donkey's a donkey. [*She looks out of the window.*] Stand still, donkey; think, Ass, you are carrying St. Christopher upon your back. Look up, Ass. Cast your eyes to Heaven. Stand absolutely still. There! I say to the Ass, look up. And the Ass looks down. The donkey is eating thistles on the lawn!

TENN.

Yes. There was a damned ass praising Browning the other day. Browning, I tell you. But I ask you, could Browning have written:

The moan of doves in immemorial elms,
The murmuring of innumerable bees.

Or this, perhaps the loveliest line in the language—The mellow ouzel fluting on the lawn? [*The donkey brays.*] Donkeys at Dimbola! Geese at Farringford! The son of man has nowhere to lay his head!

[WATTS *slowly advances into the middle.*]

16

WATTS

Praise be to the Almighty Architect—under Providence, the toe of Mammon is now, humanly speaking, in drawing. Yes, in drawing. [*He turns to them in ecstasy.*] Ah, my dear friends and fellow workers in the cause of truth which is beauty, beauty which is truth, after months of work, months of hard work, the great toe of Mammon is now in drawing. I have prayed and I have worked; I have worked and I have prayed; and humanly speaking, under Providence, the toe of Mammon is now in drawing.

TENN.

It sometimes seems to me, Watts, that the toe is not the most important part of the human body.

WATTS [*starting up and seizing his palette again*]

There speaks the voice of the true artist! You are right, Alfred. You have recalled me from my momentary exaltation. You remind me that even if I have succeeded, humanly speaking, with the great toe, I have not solved the problem of the drapery. [*He goes to the picture and takes a mahlstick.*] That indeed is a profoundly difficult problem. For by my treatment of the drapery I wish to express two important but utterly contradictory ideas. In the first place I wish to convey to the onlooker the idea that Modesty is always veiled; in the second that Modesty is absolutely naked. For a long time I have pondered at a loss. At last I have attempted a solution. I am wrapping her in a fine white substance which has the appearance of a veil; but if you examine it closely it is seen to consist of innumerable stars. It is in short the Milky Way. You ask me why? I will tell you. For if you consult the mythology of the ancient Egyptians, you will find that the Milky Way was held to symbolise— let me see, what did it symbolise— [*He opens his book.*]

MRS. C.

Let me see. Time's getting on. Now let me think. What shall I want on the voyage?

MR. C.

Faith, hope and charity.

MRS. C.

Yes and the poems of Sir Henry Taylor; and plenty of camphor. And photographs to give to the sailors.

TENN.

And a dozen or two of port.

WATTS

Horror! Horror! I have been most cruelly deceived! Listen: [*He reads.*] "The Milky Way among the ancients was the universal token of fertility. It symbolised the spawn of fish, the innumerable progeny of the sea, and the fertility of the marriage bed." Horror! Oh Horror! I who have always lived for the Utmost for the Highest have made Modesty symbolise the fertility of fish!

MR. C.

My poor old friend. Fish. Fish. Fish.

CURTAIN

18

ACT II

The Needles. ELLEN TERRY *and* JOHN CRAIG *are sitting in bathing dresses on the Needles.*

JOHN

Well, here we are!

NELL

Oh, how lovely it is to sit on a rock in the middle of the sea!

JOHN

In the middle of the sea?

NELL

Yes, it's a sea. Are you the young man who jumped over the lane on a red horse?

JOHN

I am. Are you the young woman who was picking primroses in the lane?

NELL

I am.

JOHN

[Lor'] what a lark!

21

NELL

Oh you mustn't let Signor hear you say that—or if you do, please pronounce the final *d*.

JOHN

D—be damned! Who's Signor?

NELL

Who's Signor? Oh he's the modern Titian.

JOHN

Titian?

NELL

Yes. Titian. Titian. Titian.

JOHN

Sneezing? I hope you haven't caught cold!

NELL

No. I feel heavenly. As warm as a toast—sitting in the sun here. You can't think how cold it is sitting for Modesty in a veil.

JOHN

Sitting for Modesty in a veil? What the dickens d'you mean?

NELL

Well, I'm married to a great artist. And if you're married to a great artist, you do sit for Modesty in a veil.

JOHN

Married? You're a married woman? You? Was that
old gentleman with a white beard your husband?

NELL

Oh everybody's got a white beard at Dimbola. But if
you mean, am I married to the old gentleman with a
white beard in the lane, yes, of course I am. Here's
my wedding ring. [*She pulls it off.*] With this ring
I thee wed. With this body I thee worship. Aren't you
married too?

JOHN

I married? Why I'm only twenty-two. I'm a lieutenant in the Royal Navy. That's my ship over there.
Can't you see it?

[NELL *looks.*]

NELL

That? That's a real ship. That's not the kind of ship
that sinks with all we love below the verge.

JOHN

My dear girl. I don't know what you're talking about.
Of course it's a real ship. The *Iron Duke*. Thirty-two
guns. Captain Andrew Hatch. My name's Craig. Lieutenant John Craig of Her Majesty's Navy.

NELL

And my name is Mrs. George Frederick Watts.

JOHN

But haven't you got another?

23

NELL

Oh plenty! Sometimes I'm Modesty. Sometimes I'm Poetry. Sometimes I'm Chastity. Sometimes, generally before breakfast, I'm merely Nell.

JOHN

I like Nell best.

NELL

Well that's unlucky, because today I'm Modesty. Modesty crouching at the feet of Mammon. Only Mammon's great toe was out of drawing and so I got down; and then I heard a whistle. Dear me, I suppose I'm an abandoned wretch. Everybody says how proud I ought to be. Think of hanging in the Tate Gallery for ever and ever—what an honour for a young woman like me! Only—isn't it awful—I like swimming.

JOHN

And sitting on a rock, Nell?

NELL

Well it's better than that awful model's throne. Mrs. Cameron killed the turkey today. The Muse has to have wings, you see. But you can't think how they tickle.

JOHN

What the dickens are you talking about? Who's Mrs. Cameron?

NELL

Mrs. Cameron is the photographer; and Mr. Cameron is the philosopher; and Mr. Tennyson is the poet; and

Signor is the artist. And beauty is truth; truth beauty; that is all we know and all we ought to ask. Be good, sweet maid, and let who will be clever. Oh, and the utmost for the highest, I was forgetting that.

JOHN

It's worse than shooting the sun with a sextant. Is this the Isle of Wight? Or is it the Isle of Dogs—the Isle where the mad dogs go?

NELL

The apple trees bloom all the year here; the nightingales sing all the night.

JOHN

Look here, Nell. Let's talk sense for a minute. Have you ever been in love?

NELL

In love? Aren't I married?

JOHN

Oh but like this. [*He kisses her.*]

NELL

Not quite like that. [*He kisses her again.*] But I rather like it. Of course, it must be wrong.

JOHN

Wrong? [*He kisses her.*] What's wrong about that?

NELL

It makes me think such dreadful thoughts. I don't think I could really dare to tell you. You see, it makes me think of—beef steaks; beer; standing under an umbrella in the rain; waiting to go into a theatre; crowds of people; hot chestnuts; omnibuses—all the things I've always dreamt about. And then, Signor snores. And I get up and go to the casement. And the moon's shining. And the bees on the thorn. And the dews on the lawn. And the nightingales forlorn.

JOHN

'Struth! God bless my soul! I've been in the tropics, but I've seen nothing like this. Now look here, Nell. I've got something to say to you—something very sensible. I'm not the sort of man who makes up his mind in a hurry. I took a good look at you as I jumped over that lane. And I said to myself as I landed in the turnip field, that's the girl for me. And I'm not the sort of man who does things in a hurry. Look here. [*He takes out a watch.*] Let's be married at half past two.

NELL

Married? Where shall we live?

JOHN

In Bloomsbury.

NELL

Are there any apple trees there?

JOHN

Not one.

NELL

Any nightingales?

26

JOHN

Never heard a nightingale in Bloomsbury, on my
honour as an officer.

NELL

What about painting? D'you ever paint?

JOHN

Only the bath. Red, white and blue. With Aspinalls
enamel.

NELL

But what shall we live on?

JOHN

Well, bread and butter. Sausages and kippers.

NELL

No bees. No apple trees. No nightingales. Sausages
and kippers. John, this is Heaven!

JOHN

That's fixed then. Two thirty sharp.

NELL

Oh but what about this? [*She takes her wedding ring
off.*]

JOHN

Did the old gentleman with a white beard really give
you that?

NELL

Yes. It was dug out of a tomb. Beatrice's. No, Laura's!
Lady Raven Mount Temple gave it him on the top

of the Acropolis at dawn. It symbolises—let me see, what does this wedding ring symbolise? With this ring I thee wed; with this brush I thee worship— It symbolises Signor's marriage to his art.

JOHN

He's committed bigamy. I thought so! There's something fishy about that old boy, I said to myself, as I jumped over the lane; and I'm not the sort of chap to make up his mind in a hurry.

NELL

Fishy? About Mr. Watts?

JOHN

Very fishy; yes.

[*A loud sigh is heard.*]

NELL [*looking round*]

I thought I heard somebody sighing.

JOHN [*looking round*]

I thought I saw somebody spying.

NELL

That's only one of those dreadful reporters. The beach is always full of them. They hide behind the rocks, you know, in case the Poet Laureate may be listening to the scream of the maddened beach dragged backward by the waves. [*The porpoise appears in the foreground.*] Look. Look. What's that?

JOHN

It looks to me like a porpoise.

NELL

A porpoise? A real porpoise?

JOHN

What else should a porpoise be?

NELL

Oh I don't know. But as nightingales are widows, I
thought the porpoise might be a widower. He sounds
so sad. Listen. [*The porpoise gulps.*] Oh, poor porpoise, how sad you sound! I'm sure he's hungry. Look
how his mouth opens! Haven't we anything we could
give him?

JOHN

I don't go about with my bathing drawers full of
sprats.

NELL

And I've got nothing—or only a ring. There, porpoise
—take that! [*She throws him her wedding ring.*]

JOHN

Lord, Nell! Now you've gone and done it! The porpoise has swallowed your wedding ring! What'll Lady
Mount Temple say to that?

NELL

Now you're married to Mr. Watts, porpoise! The
utmost for the highest, porpoise. Look upwards, porpoise! And keep perfectly still! I suppose it was a
female porpoise, John?

JOHN

That don't matter a damn to Mr. Watts, Nell. [*He kisses her.*]

CURTAIN

ACT III

ACT III

The studio as before. TENNYSON *reading* Maud *aloud.* TENNYSON *reads aloud for some time. Then the door opens and* WATTS *comes in, hiding his head in his hands. He staggers across the room distractedly.*

TENN.

    "The fault was mine, the fault was mine"—
    Why am I sitting here so stunn'd and still,
    Plucking the harmless wild-flower on the hill?—
    It is this guilty hand!—
    And there rises ever a passionate cry—

WATTS

    Ellen! Ellen! My wife—my wife—dead, dead, dead!

TENN.

    My God, Watts. You don't mean to say Ellen's dead?

MRS. C.

    Drowned? That's what comes of going bathing.

WATTS

    She is dead—drowned—to me. I was behind a rock on the beach. I saw her—drown.

MR. C.

    Happy Ellen! Gone to Paradise.

33

MRS. C.

Oh but this is awful! The girl's dead and where am
I to get another model for the Muse? Are you sure,
Signor, that she's quite dead? Not a spark of life left
in her? Couldn't something be done to revive her?
Brandy—where's the brandy?

WATTS

No brandy will bring Ellen to life. She is dead—stone
dead—to me.

MR. C.

Happy Ellen; lucky Ellen. They don't wear braces in
Heaven; they don't wear trousers in Heaven. Would
that I were where Ellen lies.

TENN.

Yes. There is something highly pleasing about the
death of a young woman in the pride of life. Rolled
round in earth's diurnal course with stocks and stones
and trees. That's Wordsworth. I've said it too. 'Tis
better to have loved and lost than never to have loved
at all. Wearing the white flower of a blameless life.
Hm, ha, yes let me see. Give me a pencil. Now a sheet
of paper. Alexandrines? Iambics? Sapphics? Which
shall it be?

[*He begins to write.* WATTS *goes to his canvas and
begins painting out the picture.*]

WATTS

Modesty forsooth! Chastity! Alas, I painted better
than I knew. The Ancient Egyptians were right. This

34

veil did symbolise the fertility of fish. [*He strikes his brush across it.*] What symbol can I find now?

TENN.

Ahem. I have written the first six lines. Listen. Ode on the death of Ellen Terry, a beautiful young woman who was found drowned.

[*Enter* ELLEN. *Everybody turns round in astonishment.*]

MR. C.

But you're in Heaven!

TENN.

Found drowned.

MRS. C.

Brandy's no use!

NELL

Is this a madhouse?

MR. C.

Are you a fact?

NELL

I'm Ellen Terry.

WATTS [*advancing brandishing his brush*]

Yes Ma'am. There you speak the truth. You are no longer the wife of George Frederick Watts. I saw you—

NELL

Oh you did, did you?

WATTS

I was on the beach, behind a rock. And I saw you—yes, abandoned wretch, I saw you, sitting on the Needles; sitting on the Needles with a man; sitting on the Needles with your arms round a man. This is the end, Ellen. Our marriage is dissolved—in the sea.

TENN.

The unplumb'd, salt, estranging sea. Matthew Arnold.

NELL

I'm very sorry, Signor. Indeed I am. But he looked so very hungry, Signor; I couldn't help it. *She* looked so very hungry, I should say; I'm almost sure it was a female.

WATTS

A female! Don't attempt to lie to me, Ellen.

NELL

Well, John thought it was a female. And John ought to know. John's in the Navy. He's often eaten porpoises on desert islands. Fried in oil, you know, for breakfast.

WATTS

John has eaten porpoises fried in oil for breakfast. I thought as much. Go to your lover, girl; live on porpoises fried in oil on desert islands; but leave me—to my art. [*He turns to his picture.*]

NELL

Oh well, Signor, if you will take it like that—I was only trying to cheer you up. I'm very sorry, I'm sure, to have upset you all. But I can't help it. I'm alive! I never felt more alive in all my life. But I'm awfully sorry, I'm sure—

TENN.

Don't apologise, Ellen. What does it matter? An immortal poem destroyed—that's all. [*He tears up his poem.*]

NELL

But couldn't you find a rhyme for porpoise, Mr. Tennyson?

TENN.

Impossible.

NELL

Well then, what about Craig?

TENN.

Browning could find a rhyme for Craig.

MRS. C.

Ah, but in my art rhymes don't matter. Only truth and the sun. Sit down again, Ellen. There—on that stool. Hide your head in your hands. Sob. Penitence on the stool of—

NELL [*standing at bay*]

No, I can't, Mrs. Cameron. No, I can't. First I'm Modesty; then I'm the Muse. But Penitence on a Monument—no, that I will not be.

[*a knock at the door*]

MARY

The coffins have come, Ma'am. The coffins, I say. And you couldn't find a nicer pair outside of Kensal Green. As I was saying to his lordship just now, it do seem a pity to take them all the way to India. Why can't you plant 'em here with a weeping angel on top?

MRS. C.

At last, at last the coffins have come.

MR. C.

The coffins have come.

MRS. C.

Let us pack our coffins and go.

MR. C.

To the land of perpetual moon shine—

MRS. C.

To the land where the sun never sets.

MR. C.

I shan't want trousers in India—

MRS. C.

No that's true. But I shall want wet plates—

[TENNYSON, *who has been out of the room for a moment, returns with something between his fingers.*]

TENN.

It's all right, Julia. Look. I have bored a hole with my penknife. Solid oak. Hearts of oak are our ships. Hearts

38

of oak are our men. We'll fight 'em and beat 'em
again and again! No ant can eat through that. You
can take *Maud* with you.

Well there's still time; where did I leave off? [*He
sits down and begins to read* Maud.]

> She is coming, my own, my sweet;
>> Were it ever so airy a tread,
> My heart would hear her and beat,
>> Were it earth in an earthy bed;
> My dust would hear her and beat,
>> Had I lain for a century dead;
> Would start and tremble—

MR. C. [*who is looking out of the window*]
Ahem! I think that's a fact in the raspberry canes.

TENN.
Facts? Damn facts. Facts are the death of poetry.

MR. C.
Damn facts. That is what I have always said. Plato has
said it. Radakrishna has said it. Spinoza has said it.
Confucius has said it. And Charles Hay Cameron says
it too. All the same, that was a fact in the raspberry
canes. [*Enter* CRAIG.] Are you a fact, young man?

CRAIG
My name's Craig. John Craig of the Royal Navy.
Sorry to interrupt. Afraid I've come at an incon-
venient hour. I've called to fetch Ellen by appoint-
ment.

MRS. C.
Ellen?

CRAIG

Yes. Chastity, Patience, the Muse, what d'you call her. Ah here she is.

ELLEN

John.

TENN.

Queen Rose of the rosebud garden of girls.

WATTS

Ellen, Ellen, painted, powdered. Miserable girl. I could have forgiven you much. I had forgiven you all. But now that I see you as you are—painted, powdered—unveiled—

TENN.

Remember, Watts; the ancient Egyptians said that the veil had something to do with—

WATTS

Don't bother about the ancient Egyptians now, Alfred. Now that I see you as you are, painted, powdered, I cannot do it. Vanish with your lover. Eat porpoises on desert islands.

CRAIG

Hang it all, Sir. I've a large house in Gordon Square.

WATTS

Have you indeed, Sir. And where pray is Gordon Square?

CRAIG

W.C. 1.

WATTS

Young man, have a care, have a care. Ladies are present.

CRAIG

I'm not responsible for the post office directory am I?

TENN.

Hallam lived there. Wimpole Street, West Central, we called it in those more euphonious days. The long unlovely street. See *In Memoriam*.

CRAIG

What's Hallam? What's *In Memoriam?*

TENN.

What's Hallam? What's *In Memoriam?* It is time I went back to Farringford. Emily will be anxious.

NELL

Take care Emily don't jump, Mr. Tennyson!

[*Enter* MARY.]

MARY

The coffins are on the fly, Ma'am.

MRS. C.

The coffins are on the fly— It is time to say good-bye.

MARY

There's no room for the turkey's wings, Ma'am.

MRS. C.

Give them here. I will put them in my reticule.

MARY

Gorblime! What a set! What a set! Coffins in the kitchen. Wet plates on the mantelpiece. And when you go to pick up a duster, it's a marmoset. I'm sick of parlour work. I'll marry the earl and live like a respectable gurl in a Castle.

MR. AND MRS. C., JOHN AND ELLEN [*all together*]

The coffins are on the fly. It's time to say good-bye.

MRS. C.

We are going to the land of the sun.

MR. C.

We are going to the land of the moon.

JOHN

We're going to W.C. 1.

NELL

Thank God we're going soon.

MRS. C.

Good-bye, good-bye, the coffins are on the fly.

MR. C.

Farewell to Dimbola; Freshwater, farewell.

JOHN

I say, Nell, I want a rhyme to fly.

NELL

Heavens, John, I can only think of fly.

MRS. C.

    And my message to my age is
    When you want to take a picture
    Be careful to fix your
    Lens out of focus.

But what's a rhyme to focus?

MR. C.

    Hocus pocus, hocus pocus,
    That's the rhyme to focus.
    And my message to my age is—
    Watts—don't keep marmosets in cages—

JOHN AND NELL

  They're all cracked—quite cracked—

    And our message to our age is,
    If you want to paint a veil,
    Never fail,
    To look in the raspberry canes for a fact.

NELL

  To look in the raspberry canes for a fact!

[*Exeunt all but* WATTS *and* TENNYSON.]

TENN.

  They have left us, Watts.

WATTS

  Alone with our art.

TENN. [*going to the window*]

  Low on the sand and loud on the stone the last wheel

43

echoes away. God bless my soul, it don't! It's getting louder—louder—louder! They're coming back!

WATTS

Don't tell me, Alfred! Don't tell me they're coming back! I couldn't face another—fact!

TENN.

She is coming, my dove, my dear;
    She is coming, my life, my fate.
The red rose cries, "She is near, she is near"—

MARY

Her Majesty the Queen.

THE QUEEN

We have arrived. We are extremely pleased to see you both. We prefer to stand. It is the anniversary of our wedding day. Ah, Albert! And in token of that never to be forgotten, always to be remembered, ever to be lamented day—

TENN.

'Tis better to have loved and lost.

THE QUEEN

Ah but you are both so happily married. We have brought you these tokens of our regard. To you, Mr. Tennyson, a peerage. To you, Mr. Watts, the Order of Merit. May the spirit of the blessed Albert look down and preserve us all.

CURTAIN

44

NOTES

[*1935 Version*]

Act One

The setting is Dimbola, the Cameron home at Freshwater Bay on the Isle of Wight. Virginia condenses the time of the action, for in actuality Ellen Terry and Watts ended their marriage in 1865, the Camerons left England with their coffins in 1875, and Tennyson accepted the peerage in 1884. Most references in the play are biographically accurate. An important exception is Ellen Terry's romantic escapade with John Craig. A minor exception is the Camerons' destination. They sailed to Ceylon rather than to the more euphonious "India."

Virginia wrote a short historical sketch of Julia Cameron for the 1926 Hogarth Press publication *Victorian Photographs of Famous Men and Fair Women.*

"Sit still, Charles" (page 7).

In one of several early versions of her short story "The Searchlight," Virginia humorously describes the efficiency with which Mrs. Cameron, with clenched fist and threats of damnation, forced those around her to sit still. Virginia incorporated a number of ideas and passages from these manuscripts, now at the University of Sussex Library, into *Freshwater.*

"Surely you can put up with a little discomfort in the cause of art" (page 7).

45

When doing a picture entitled "Despair," Mrs. Cameron is said to have locked her model in a closet for several hours in order to get the right expression on her face. See Brian Hill, *Julia Margaret Cameron: A Victorian Family Portrait.*

Watts and Tennyson were two of Mrs. Cameron's closest friends and advisors. She moved to Freshwater in 1860 to be near the Tennyson home at Farringford during her husband's absence in Ceylon.

"A philosopher with his beard dipped in moonlight" (page 7).

Tennyson used just these words in describing Mr. Cameron. See *Alfred, Lord Tennyson: A Memoir by His Son.*

"The Utmost for the Highest" (page 8).

The phrase was Watts's motto. See Mary Seton Watts, *George Frederick Watts: Annals of an Artist's Life*, a book Virginia mentions in her diary on 30 January 1919. This is the same entry in which she first discusses her plans for *Freshwater.*

"six American professors are in the summer house" (page 8).

Tennyson's son records this incident.

"the Earl of Dudley" (page 9).

Mrs. Cameron's maid, model, and photographic assistant did in fact marry a peer, although not the Earl of Dudley. Virginia's choice of this title may suggest a family joke, since Mrs. Cameron's great-niece married the second Earl of Dudley. Henry Taylor's *Autobiography* gives a humorous account of Mary's rise from rags to riches under Mrs. Cameron's tutelage.

"he's a deal sight better than coffins any day" (page 9).

The manuscript reads "del" for "deal."

"When we lie . . . my head will be pillowed" (page 9).

Vanessa Bell's notes correct an apparent typographical error here. Virginia's manuscript reads "my heart will be pillowed."

"Oh, Signor" (page 10).

The notes to Ellen Terry's *Memoirs*, edited by Edith Craig and Christopher St. John and published in 1933, give this picture of her status as Watts's sixteen-year-old wife: " 'The Signor,' as Watts was called by his friends, was surrounded by a little court of married women of his own age . . . who seemed to have made it their business to keep his child-wife in order. She was subjected to a humiliating surveillance and had strict injunction not to open her mouth in the presence of distinguished guests."

Ellen Terry's autobiography reveals how demanding her first husband could be: "I remember sitting to him in armour for hours and never realising that it was heavy until I fainted."

"I am not yet a Lord, damsel" (page 11).

The manuscript offers two choices in Tennyson's reply to Ellen's "Oh Lord, Lord, Lord!": 1) "That may lie

47

on the lap of the Gods." The word "knee" is deleted.
2) "That may lie on the lap of the Queen." Queen seems
the sensible choice in view of the Queen's entrance at the
close of the play. Vanessa Bell's note for Tennyson's re-
mark "Meanwhile, sit on *my* lap" reads "on my knee."

"Here's the turkey wings" (page 13).

This was originally Mary's speech. The manuscript
here is scrambled.

"The turkey has become part and parcel of my immortal
art" (page 14).

Mrs. Cameron continually claimed to have "immortal-
ized" her subjects.

"Come, my marmoset" (page 14).

Virginia's handwritten cast list includes "Mitzi,"
Leonard Woolf's pet marmoset. Since the monkey was a
resident of Monk's House in 1935, this further supports the
dating of this manuscript. Vanessa Bell's handwritten cast
list does not include the roles of porpoise and marmoset
and casts "JB" (Julian Bell) as Lord Tennyson, "Ann"
(Ann Stephen) as John Craig, and "Eve" (Eve Younger)
as Mary. Mrs. Ann Stephen Synge remembers her father,
Adrian Stephen, in the role of Tennyson and is certain
that she did not play a man; no one else interviewed
recalls a woman playing a man's role in the 1935 performance.

"Why did I say 'rosy'? Because it is a fact—" (page 15).

Ruskin singled out this line as a "pathetic fallacy."
Thomas Wilson in *Reminiscence* quotes Tennyson as

follows: "Why the very day I wrote it, I saw the daisies rosy in Maiden's Croft, and thought of enclosing one to Ruskin labelled 'A Pathetic Fallacy.' "

"The donkey is eating thistles on the lawn" (page 16).

There follows the deleted line: "There are moments when I despair of modern life altogether."

"The moan of doves . . . innumerable bees" (page 16).

These two lines are from Tennyson's *The Princess: A Medley*. The second line should read "And murmuring . . ."

"The mellow ouzel . . ." (page 16).

This is from "The Gardener's Daughter." The correct line reads "The mellow ouzel fluted in the elm."

Following the stage directions for Watts to open his book (page 18), Virginia deletes the following passage:

MRS. C.

> Come here, Charles. Let me dry your head. Let Julia Margaret Cameron work up to the last moment in the service of her art. [*She dries him.*] All my sisters were beautiful, but I had genius. They were the brides of men; but I am the bride of art. I have sought beauty in public houses. I have found her playing the concertina in the street. My housemaid sold bootlaces at Charing Cross; she is now the wife of the Earl of Dudley; my bootboy stole eggs and was in prison; he now waits at table in the guise of Cupid. I have sought beauty in the most unlikely places—

We find this passage in an expanded form in the earlier version of *Freshwater* (see pages 64–65).

"Sir Henry Taylor" (page 18).

Another close friend of Mrs. Cameron, he appears in Virginia's early drafts of "The Searchlight" manuscripts.

"I . . . have made Modesty symbolise the fertility of fish" (page 18).

Watts emphasized throughout his life that art in its highest form is always symbolic.

Following Mr. Cameron's closing line in Act One (page 18), these final passages have been deleted:

TENN.
> That's what comes of toying with symbols. I have always said, take care of the sound and the sense will take care of itself.

MRS. C.
> Oh Signor, Signor! You have made Modesty symbolise the fertility of fish.

ALL THREE [*speaking together*]
> Signor has made Modesty symbolise the fertility of fish!

David Richman, director of a production of *Freshwater* at Stanford University in 1974, reinstated the above passage to help support what he terms the musical structure of the play: "Not only does the play have an operatic quality; the structure of the three acts is much like that of a symphonic composition. The fast-paced first and third acts are similar in their abundance of thematic material to the outer movements of a classical symphony. The middle act, a lyric section which focuses on Ellen Terry and her lover, is in the nature of an andante." "Directing Freshwater," *Virginia Woolf Miscellany*, Spring, 1974.

Act Two

"The Needles" (page 21).

This refers to a group of chalk rocks off the southwest coast of the Isle of Wight.

"John Craig" (page 21).

Virginia's naval lieutenant is apparently fictional. Ellen Terry's two children by Edward Godwin, with whom she lived briefly after her separation from Watts, were subsequently given the legal name Craig.

The only man who ever jumped over her head on horseback, however, seems to have been playwright Charles Reade, the friend who was responsible for bringing Ellen Terry back into the theatre.

"[Lor'] what a lark" (page 21).

The manuscript reads simply "I say, what a lark!" Nell's response suggests an omitted phrase.

"Titian" (page 22).

Titian was one of Watts's favorite painters.

"Is this the Isle of Wight" (page 25).

Nell's reply to John's question is scrambled and hard to decipher from the manuscript corrections.

"And the nightingales forlorn" (page 26).

This phrase occurs in "The Searchlight" manuscript along with a number of bird images that appear in *Freshwater*.

Act Three

"Yes. There is something highly pleasing . . . in the pride of life" (page 34).

"Pride" may be a typographical error for "prime."

"a beautiful young woman who was found drowned" (page 35).

Found Drowned is the title of a painting by Watts. His wife described it as "the wreck of a young girl's life." Ellen Terry left a two-word note, "Found Drowned," attached to a photograph of Watts when in 1868 she ran off with Godwin.

"Browning could find a rhyme for Craig" (page 37).

Tennyson's son records a conversation between his father and Browning in which the latter claimed "that he could make a rhyme for every word in the English language."

APPENDIX

FRESHWATER

A Comedy

[1923 Version]

Dramatis Personae
CHARLES HENRY HAY CAMERON
MRS. JULIA CAMERON
G. F. WATTS
ELLEN TERRY
LORD TENNYSON
MR. CRAIG
MARY MAGDALEN

A drawing room at Dimbola, hung with photographs; CHARLES
CAMERON, *a very old man with long white hair and beard, is
sitting with a bath towel round his head.* MARY MAGDALEN, *the
housemaid, is engaged in rubbing his hair, which has just been
washed, and is of the utmost fineness.*

MR. C.

The sixth time in eight months! Whenever we start for
India, Julia insists—[*Here* MARY, *who is combing, tugs
his hair sharply.*]—Ah! Ah! Ah!—Julia insists that I must
have my head washed. Yet we never do start for India—I
sometimes think we never shall start for India. At the last
moment something happens—something always happens.
And so we stay on and on, living this life of poetry, of
photography, of frivolity, and I shall never see the land of
my spiritual youth. I shall never learn the true nature of
virtue from the fasting philosophers of Baluchistan. I shall
never solve the great problem, or answer the Eternal Ques-

55

tion. I am a captive in the hands of Circumstance—
[MARY *now tugs his beard.*] Ah! Oh! Oh!

MARY

Mr. Cameron, dear darling Mr. Cameron, do let me wash
your beard. It's the most beautiful beard in the whole Isle
of Wight. Mrs. Cameron will never let you go to India—

[*Enter* MRS. CAMERON, *a brown-faced gipsylike-looking old
woman, wearing a green shawl, fastened by an enormous
cameo. She stops dead and raises her hand.*]

MRS. C.

What a picture! What a composition! Truth sipping at the
fount of inspiration! The soul taking flight from the body!
Upward, girl, look upward! Fling your arms round his
neck and look upward! [MARY *and* MR. C. *assume a pose.*]
Let your head fall on your breast, Charles. The soul has left
its mortal tenement. She wings her way—where are the
wings, the angel's wings, the turkey's wings, Andrews gave
me last Christmas?

MARY

They're packed, ma'am.

MRS. C.

Packed—why packed? Ah—I remember. We start for
India at two thirty sharp. [MARY *goes on combing the
beard.*] Did you ever hear anything so provoking? I've
only just time to finish my study of Sir Galahad watching
the Holy Grail by moonlight. Cook was posed. The light
superb. At the last moment up comes word that Galahad
has to take the sheep to Yarmouth. It's market day. Sheep!
Market day! [*With great scorn*] Where I'm to find another
Galahad heaven only knows! [*She looks distractedly about
the room, out of the window and so on.*]

56

MR. C. [*lying back with his eyes shut, while* MARY *washes his beard*]

Loose your mind from the affairs of the present. Seek truth where truth lies hidden. Follow the everlasting will o' the wisp—Magdalen, don't tug my beard. Cast away your vain fineries. Let us be free like birds of the air. [*Growing more and more excited, and speaking in a loud prophetic voice*] At two thirty we start for India!

[*The door opens as he says this and* LORD TENNYSON *enters.*]

LORD T.

So Emily told me. Julia Cameron has ordered the coffins, she said, and at two thirty they start for India.

MRS. C. [*advancing upon him and speaking in a sepulchral voice*]

Julia Cameron has ordered the coffins but the coffins have not come. It's that villain Ashwood again. This is the sixth time I have ordered the coffins and the coffins have not come. But without her coffins Julia Cameron will not start for India. For, Alfred [*she stands before him, fixing him with her eyes*], when we lie dead under the Southern Cross, my head will be raised upon a copy of *In Memoriam. Maud* lies upon my heart. In my right hand I hold the quill which wrote—under providence—"The Passing of Arthur." In my left, the slipper which you threw at my head when I asked you to sit for my two hundredth study of Arthur saying farewell to Sir Bedivere. [*She casts her eyes up and speaks in a deep ecstatic voice.*] All is over, Alfred. All is ready. It is a deep Southern night. Orion glitters in the firmament. The scent of the tulip trees is wafted through the open window. The silence is only broken by the sobs of my faithful friends and the occasional howl of a solitary tiger. And then—what is this?

What infamy is this? [*She plucks at her wrist, picks something off it, and holds it towards* TENNYSON.] An Ant! A White Ant! They are advancing in hordes from the jungle, Alfred. I hear the crepitation of their myriad feet. They will be upon me before dawn. They will eat the flesh off my bones. Alfred, they will devour *Maud!*

LORD T. [*greatly shocked*]

God bless my soul! The woman's right. Devour *Maud!* It's too disgusting! It must be stopped. Devour *Maud* indeed! My darling *Maud!* [*He presses the book beneath his arm.*] But what an awful fate! What a hideous prospect! Here are my two honoured old friends, setting sail, in less than three hours, for an unknown land where, whatever else may happen, they can never by any possible chance hear me read *Maud* again. But [*he looks at his watch*] what is the time? We have still two hours and twenty minutes. I have read it in less. Let us begin. [LORD TENNYSON *sits down by the window which opens into the garden and begins to read aloud.*]

> I hate the dreadful hollow beneath the little wood,
>   Its lips in the field above are dabbled with blood-red
>   heath,
>   The red-ribb'd ledges drip with a silent horror
>   of blood,
>   And Echo there, whatever is ask'd her, answers
>   "Death."

MRS. C. [*interrupting him*]

Alfred, Alfred, I seek Sir Galahad. Where shall I find a Galahad? Is there no gardener, no footman, no pantry boy at Farringford with calves—he must have calves. Hallam alas has grown too stout. A Galahad! A Galahad! [*She goes wringing her hands and crying "A Galahad!" out of the room.* TENNYSON *goes on reading steadily.*]

58

LORD T.

> For there in the ghastly pit long since a body was
>   found,
> His who had given me life—O father! O God! was
>   it well?—
> Mangled, and flatten'd, and crush'd, and dinted
>   into the ground;
> There yet lies the rock that fell with him when
>   he fell.

[TENNYSON *becomes absorbed in his reading and does not notice that* [illegible]. MR. CAMERON *falls asleep and snores gently.* TENNYSON *goes on reading. The door opens and* ELLEN TERRY *comes in, dressed in white veils which are wrapped about her arms, head, etc.* TENNYSON *reads on to himself in rather a low voice, without noticing her.* MR. CAMERON *snores very quietly.*]

ELLEN [*looking from one to the other*]

O how usual it all is. Nothing ever changes in this house. Somebody's always asleep. Lord Tennyson is always reading *Maud*. The cook is always being photographed. The Camerons are always starting for India. I'm always sitting to Signor. I'm Modesty today—Modesty crouching at the feet of Mammon. If it weren't for Mammon, I should be there still. But Mammon's big toe is out of drawing. Of course Signor with all his high ideals couldn't pass that. So I slipped down and escaped. If I only *could* escape. [*She wrings her hands in desperation.*] For I never thought when I married Mr. Watts that it was going to be like this. I thought artists were such jolly people—always dressing up and hiring coaches and going for picnics and drinking champagne and eating oysters and kissing each other and—well, behaving like the Rossettis. As it is, Signor can't eat anything except the gristle of beef minced very fine and passed through the kitchen chopper twice. He drinks a glass of hot water at nine and goes to bed in woolen socks at nine thirty sharp. Instead of kissing me he gives me a white rose every morning. Every morning he says the same thing—"The Utmost for the Highest, Ellen! The Utmost for the Highest!" And so of course I have to sit to him all day long. Everybody says how proud I must be to hang for ever and ever in the Tate Gallery as Modesty crouching beneath the feet of Mammon. But I'm an abandoned wretch, I suppose. I have such awful thoughts. Sometimes I actually want to go upon the stage and be an actress. What would Signor say if he knew? And then, when I'm dressed like this, all in white and crouching there under Mammon's big toe, it suddenly comes into my head that I should like somebody to fall in love with me. And, what's much worse—oh, it's so unspeakable that I can't think how I've the face to go on crouching any longer —somebody *has* fallen in love with me. At least I think so. It happened like this. Signor and I were picking primroses in Maidens Lane. Suddenly I heard the sound of galloping hoofs, and a horse and rider sprang right over our heads. Luckily, the lane was very deep, or we should have been killed. Luckily, Signor is very deaf and he heard nothing. But I had just time to see a beautiful, sunburnt, whiskered face and to catch this. [*She takes out a piece of paper and reads.*]

> Come into the garden, Nell,
> I'm here at the gate alone.
> Tuesday, Midday, Craig.

Tuesday! Midday! Craig! It is Tuesday. [*She goes up to the mantelpiece and looks at the large ticking clock.*] It is just half past eleven. But who's Craig?

LORD T. [*bursting out in great agitation*]
Colvin has the temerity to say that my lyrics are better than my narrative. Gosse has the audacity to affirm that my narrative is better than my lyrics. That is the kind of

criticism I have to endure. That is my daily portion of insult and injustice. If I weren't the most stoical man in the world, the very skin on my wrists would rise and blossom in purple and red at the innumerable bites of the poisoned bugs and pismires of the Press! [*He shoots out his hand and looks at it.*] That's a wonderful hand now. The skin is like a crumpled rose leaf. Young woman [*beckoning to* ELLEN], have you ever seen a poet's skin?—a great poet's skin? Ah, you should see me in my bath! I have thighs like alabaster.

ELLEN

It's a very beautiful skin, Lord Tennyson.

LORD T.

And you're a very beautiful wench. Get on my knee.

ELLEN

I sometimes think you're the most sensible of them all, Lord Tennyson.

LORD T. [*kissing her*]

I am sensible to beauty in all its shapes. That is my function as Poet Laureate.

ELLEN

Tell me, Lord Tennyson, have *you*—ever picked primroses?

LORD T.

Millions and millions of times.

ELLEN

And did Lady Tennyson ever jump over your head?

LORD T.

Jump! Emily jump! She has lain on her sofa for fifty years.

She took to it on her honeymoon, and I should be surprised, indeed I should be shocked, if she ever got up again.

ELLEN

Then I suppose you were never in love. You were never in the devil of a mess. Nobody ever painted you in your chemise. Nobody ever gave you a white rose. Nobody ever threw a note into your hand and galloped away.

LORD T.

No: Hallam never galloped. He had a bad seat on horseback. My life has been singularly free from amorous excitement of the kind you describe. Tell me more.

ELLEN

If you were quite young and you saw somebody you wanted to marry and she was married already to an old, old man, would you throw everything to the winds— your name, your fame, your house, your books, your servants, your wife—and elope with her?

LORD T. [*in great agitation*]
I should! I should!

ELLEN

Thank you, Lord Tennyson. You're a very great poet! [*She kisses him, slips off his knee and runs out of the room.*]

MR. C. [*opening his eyes slowly*]
Alfred, Alfred!

LORD T. [*much startled*]
I thought you were asleep!

MR. C.

It is when our eyes are shut that we see most!

LORD T.

But there is no need to mention it to Emily.

MR. C. [*dreamily*]

I slept, and had a vision. I thought I was looking into the
future. I saw a yellow omnibus advancing down the glades
of Farringford. I saw girls with red lips kissing young men
without shame. I saw innumerable pictures of innumerable
apples. Girls played games. Great men were no longer
respected. Purity had fled from the hearth. The double
bed had shrunk to a single. Yet as I wandered, lost, be-
wildered, utterly confounded, through the halls of Alfred
Tennyson's home, I felt my youth return. My eyes cleared,
my hair turned black, my powers revived. And [*trembling
and stretching his arms out*] there was a damsel—an
exquisite but not altogether ethereal nymph. Her name
was Lydia. She was a dancer. She came from Muscovy.
She had danced before the Tsar. She snatched me by the
waist and whirled me through the currant bushes. Oh
Alfred, Alfred, tell me, was it but a dream?

[*Enter* GEORGE FREDERICK WATTS *carrying a palette.*]

WATTS

Where is Ellen? Has anybody seen Ellen? She must have
slipped from the room without my noticing it. [*Turning to
the audience and speaking in rapturous tones*] Praise be
to the Almighty Architect! The toe of Mammon is now,
speaking under Providence, in drawing. Ah, my dear old
friends, that toe has meant months of work—months of
hard work. I have allowed myself no relaxation. I have
sustained my body on the gristle of beef passed through
the kitchen chopper twice, and my soul by the repetition
of one prayer—The Utmost for the Highest! The Utmost
for the Highest. At last my prayer has been heard; my
request granted. The toe, the big toe, is now in drawing.
[*He sits down.*]

LORD T. [*gloomily*]

It sometimes seems to me that the toe is not the most important part of the human body, Watts.

WATTS [*starting up*]

There speaks the voice of the true artist. You are right, Alfred. You have recalled me from my exaltation; upwards, you point upwards. You remind me that even if I have succeeded, humanly speaking, with the toe, I have not solved the problem of the drapery. That, indeed, is a profoundly difficult problem. For by my treatment of the drapery I wish to express two distinct and utterly contradictory ideas. In the first place it should convey to the onlooker the idea that Modesty is always veiled; in the second, that Modesty is absolutely naked. For a long time I have pondered at a loss. At last I have solved the problem. I am wrapping her form in a fine white substance, which has the appearance of a veil but, if you examine it closely, is seen to consist of innumerable stars. It is, in short, the Milky Way. For in the Mythology of Ancient Egypt the Milky Way was held to symbolise—let me see, what did it symbolise?— [*He searches in his pockets and takes out a large book.*]

[*Enter* MRS. CAMERON *with her camera.*]

MRS. C.

What is the use of a policeman if he has no calves? There you have the tragedy of my life. That is Julia Margaret Cameron's message to her age! [*She sits down facing the audience.*] All my sisters were beautiful, but I had genius [*touching her forehead*]. They were the brides of men, but I am the bride of Art. I have sought the beautiful in the most unlikely places. I have searched the police force at Freshwater, and not a man have I found with calves worthy of Sir Galahad. But, as I said to the Chief Constable, "Without beauty, constable, what is order? Without life,

64

what is law?" Why should I continue to have my silver protected by a race of men whose legs are aesthetically abhorrent to me? If a burglar came and he were beautiful, I should say to him: Take my fish knives! Take my cruets, my bread baskets and my soup tureens. What you take is nothing to what you give, your calves, your beautiful calves. I have sought beauty in public houses and found her playing the concertina in the street. My cook was a mendicant. I have transformed her into a Queen. My house-maid sold bootlaces at Charing Cross; she is now engaged to the Earl of Dudley. My bootboy stole eggs and was in prison. He now waits at table in the guise of Cupid.

WATTS [*crying out in agony*]

Horror! Horror! I have been cruelly misled—utterly deceived. [*He reads aloud.*] "The Milky Way among the Ancient Egyptians was the universal token of fertility. It symbolised the spawn of fish, the innumerable progeny of the sea, and the harvest of the fields. It typified the fertility of the marriage bed, and its blessings were called down upon brides at the altar." Horror! Horror! I who have always lived for the Utmost for the Highest have made Modesty symbolise the fertility of fish! My picture is ruined! I must start afresh. It will cost me months of work, but it must be done. It shall never be said that George Frederick Watts painted a single hair that did not tend directly—or indirectly—to the spiritual and moral elevation of the British Public. Where is Ellen? There is not a moment to be lost. The Utmost for the Highest! The Utmost for the Highest!

MR. C.

Where is Ellen, Alfred?

LORD T.

Where is Lydia, Charles?

65

MRS. C.

Who is Lydia?

LORD T.

Who is Lydia, what is she that all our swains adore her?

MR. C.

She is a Muscovite. She danced before the Tsar.

MRS. C.

The very person I want! A housemaid who can dance!

WATTS

I have been visited by a most marvellous inspiration. Why should I not transform Modesty into Maternity? I see no treachery to the British Public in that. Mammon trampling upon Maternity. The sound is certainly excellent; but what about the sense?

LORD T.

Take care of the sound and the sense will take care of itself.

WATTS [*fumbling in his pocket and producing several papers*]
I must make sure of my facts this time. I have here a letter from Rosalind, Countess of Carlisle, a very noble and high-minded lady whom I am even now painting as Boadicea or Godiva—I forget which—but here it is. She is profoundly interested in the suppression of the sale of spirituous liquors—a movement which has my fullest sympathy; but hitherto, owing partly to the pressure of other subjects, I have not devised any means of treating a glass of hot water allegorically. [*He reads.*] "Dearest Signor, great painter of all time, brother of Michael Angelo, son of Titian, nephew of Tintoret, you who wear the white flower of a blameless Art, will scarcely credit the fact that the Working Classes of Great Britain spend upon beer in one

66

year a sum sufficient to maintain and equip twenty battle-ships or two million horse marines." No; that had never struck me. Never! But there is my picture! Lady Carlisle has given me my picture! Mammon typifies British love of beer. Maternity, two million horse marines. The Milky Way symbolising the spawn of fish and the fertility of the marriage bed may be held, without impropriety, to be highly symbolical of two million horse marines. Thus the picture will serve I hope a very high and holy purpose. I shall call it Mammon trampling upon Maternity, or the Prosperity of the British Empire being endangered—

LORD T. [*interrupting*]
—by the fertility of the Horse Marines.

WATTS
No, no, no, Alfred. You mistake my meaning entirely. I shall call it Mammon trampling upon Maternity or the Prosperity of the British Empire being endangered by the addiction of the Working Classes to the Consumption of Spirituous Liquors—

LORD T. [*shrieking and clasping his head*]
Oh, oh, oh—twelve *s*'es in ten lines—twelve *s*'es in ten lines! The pro*sss*perity of the Briti*sss*h—the *sss*pawn of the Horse Marines—con*sss*umption of *sss*pirituous fi*sss*hes—Oh, oh, oh, I feel faint! [*He sinks onto the table.*]

MRS. C. [*planting her tripod*]
"The Passing of Arthur!"

WATTS [*going up to* TENNYSON *and patting him on the shoulder*]
Cheer up, my dear old friend; cheer up. I will be guided entirely by your wishes. I will call it merely "Mammon

67

trampling upon Maternity." Unless I mistake—and I have made some very terrible mistakes today—there is not a single letter *s* in the line.

LORD T.

The moan of doves in immemorial elms. The murmuring of innumerable bees. Myriads of rivulets hurrying through the lawns. Forgive my weakness. It is years since I encountered the letter *s* in such profusion. Hallam eradicates them from the *Times* with a penknife every morning. Even so, the Siege of Sevastopol was almost the death of me. If I had not been engaged in writing *Maud* at the time, I doubt that I could have survived. Living at Farringford there is constant danger from flocks of geese. So I carry a copy of my own works wherever I go and fortify myself by repeating the mellow ouzel fluting on the lawn, the moan of doves in immemorial elms. Maud, Maud, Maud, they are crying and calling. Maud, Maud, Maud. [*He sits down by the window and begins to read.*]

MRS. C. [*fluttering her fingers*]

"Inspiration—or the poet's dream." Look at the outline of the nose against the ivy! Look at the hair tumbling like Atlantic billows on a stormy night! And the eyes—look up, Alfred, look up—they are like pools of living light in which thoughts play like dolphins among groves of coral. The legs are a trifle short, but legs, thank God, can always be covered. [*She covers his legs with an embroidered table cloth.*] Charles, rouse yourself. Signor, lean against the window frame. Cook! Louisa! Mary Magdalen! James! Lord Tennyson is about to read *Maud*.

[*The servants come trooping in,* COOK *dressed as Guenevere;* JAMES *as Cupid. They form a tableau round* LORD TENNYSON *at the window.*]

MRS. C. [*to the audience*]

"Alfred, Lord Tennyson reading *Maud* to Julia Margaret Cameron for the last time."

LORD T.

Come into the garden, Nell,
[*The clock begins striking twelve as he reads.*]
I am here at the gate alone;
And the woodbine spices are wafted abroad,
And the musk of the rose is blown.

She is coming, my own, my dear;
Were it ever so airy a tread,
My heart would hear her and beat,
Were it earth in an earthy bed;
My dust would hear her and beat,
Had I lain for a century dead;
Would start and tremble under her feet,
And blossom in purple and red.

MRS. C. [*in great excitement, pointing at the window*]

Sir Galahad!

ALL

Sir Galahad?

MRS. C.

There among the raspberry canes—kissing; no, being kissed. Wait, young man. Wait! [*She dashes out of the room.*]

MR. C.

I slept, and had a vision in my sleep. I saw a yellow omnibus advancing down the glade. I saw Lydia among the raspberry canes.

69

WATTS

Your music, Alfred, has tuned my mind to its highest pitch, and I now feel inspired to approach the most awful problems of my art in a spirit of devout devotion. But where is Ellen? I must find Ellen. Where is Ellen?

[*Enter* MRS. CAMERON *with* ELLEN TERRY, *who is dressed as a young man.*]

MRS. C.

I have found him at last. Sir Galahad!

[*Everybody stares.* WATTS, TENNYSON *and* MR. CAMERON *rise to their feet.*]

LORD T.

Nell!

MR. C.

Lydia!

WATTS

Ellen! Oh, Modesty, Modesty. [*He sinks down covering his face with his hand.*]

MRS. C.

Why, it's Ellen Terry dressed up as a man. How becoming trousers are, to be sure! I have never, never, seen anything so exquisite as Ellen in the arms of a youth among the raspberry canes.

WATTS [*starting up*]

In the arms of a youth! In trousers in the arms of a youth! My wife in trousers in the arms of a youth! Unmaidenly! Unchaste! Impure! Out of my sight! Out of my life!

[*Enter* MR. CRAIG.]

70

CRAIG

And into my arms. Come along, Nell. It's time we were off. You can't keep a horse tied up at the gate all day in this weather.

MR. C.

I slept, and had a vision in my sleep. I thought I saw a motor omnibus advancing down the glades of Farringford. What colour is your horse, young Sir?

CRAIG

A strawberry roan.

MR. C.

Then my dream has come—more or less—true. The omnibus was yellow.

WATTS

Miserable girl—if girl I still can call you. I could have forgiven you much but not this. Had you gone to meet him as a maiden, in a veil, or dressed in white, it would have been different. But trousers—no—check trousers; no. Go then. Vanish with your paramour to lead a life of corruption.

CRAIG

Hang it all, Sir. I have a large house in Gordon Square.

WATTS

Go then to Gordon Square. Found a society in which the sanctity of the marriage vow is no longer respected, where veils are rent and trousers, check trousers—

ELLEN

O, I was forgetting. [*She pulls a long veil out of her pocket.*] Here's your veil. I intend to wear trousers in future. I never could understand the sense of wearing veils in a climate like this.

WATTS

Unhappy maiden. You have no ideals. No imagination. No religion. No sense of the symbolical in art. The veil which you cast asunder symbolises purity, modesty, chastity—

LORD T.

—and the fertility of fish. Don't forget that, Watts.

ELLEN [*to* CRAIG]

I don't understand a word they're saying. But then I never did. Can't we escape to some place where people talk sense?

WATTS

Go to Bloomsbury. In that polluted atmosphere spread your doctrines, propagate your race, wear your trousers. But there will come a day [*he raises his eyes and clasps his hands*] when the voice of purity, of conscience, of highmindedness, of nobility, and truth, will again be heard in the land.

MR. C. [*gazing in front of him as if at a vision*]

The reference is to Middleton Murry and the *Adelphi*. All expectations have been surpassed. You are urgently advised to secure advertising space without delay. Highmindedness pays.

WATTS

Thank God for that! It was not so in my day. To this Middleton Murry, then, I bequeath my mantle. [*He flourishes the veil.*] As for you [*turning upon* ELLEN *and* MR. CRAIG] guilty, unbridled, unhallowed couple, fly!

[*The door opens, and undertakers carry in two coffins which they put down in the middle of the room.*]

72

MRS. C.

They have come. They have come!

MR. C.

At last, at last! We start for India. [MR. *and* MRS. CAMERON *clasp hands and stand by the coffins.*]

MR. AND MRS. C.

We start for India. We go to seek a land less corrupted by hypocrisy, where nature prevails. A land where the sun always shines. Where philosophers speak the truth. Where men are naked. Where women are beautiful. Where damsels dance among the currant bushes— It is time— It is time. We go; we go.

ELLEN AND MR. CRAIG

And we go too. We go to a land—

ELLEN

Oh I've had enough of this style of talking! The fact is we're going to Bloomsbury—number forty-six Gordon Square, W.C. 1. There won't be no veils there! Not if I know it!

MR. C. [*walking slowly out of the room with his hands stretched before him*]

Lydia—Lydia—I come—I come!

MRS. C. [*running back into the room*]

Wait, wait. I have left my camera behind. [*She takes it and holds it towards* ELLEN TERRY.] It is my wedding gift, Ellen. Take my lens. I bequeath it to my descendents. See that it is always slightly out of focus. Farewell! Farewell!

[*Exeunt* MR. *and* MRS. CAMERON *and* ELLEN *and* CRAIG. *A noise of shouting is heard, which dies away and grows again. Excited servants rush in.*]

73

SERVANTS

It is the Queen, my Lord! She has driven over from Balmoral to see you.

[HER MAJESTY QUEEN VICTORIA *is wheeled in in an arm chair.*]

WATTS [*falling on his knees at her feet*]
The Utmost for the Highest!

LORD T. [*to the audience, very grimly*]
The comedy is over.

[LORD TENNYSON *falls on his knees. Several gramophones play "God Save the Queen," and the curtain falls.*]

NOTES

[*1923 Version*]

Virginia's 1923 letter to Desmond MacCarthy (see Preface) describes the play as having six parts. "Lydia, Adrian, Nessa," she writes, "are already cast. The rest await your decision." That seven parts are listed in this manuscript is an interesting discrepancy. Another discrepancy in this letter regards Virginia's description of the play as "a skit upon our great aunts." While the reference to "aunts" may be simply an irrelevant slip, it might also suggest that she wrote another as yet undiscovered version of *Freshwater*.

"Mary Magdalen" (page 55).

Most likely the character here is based on Mrs. Cameron's maid, Mary Hillier, known as "Mary Madonna" or "Island Mary" because she posed so frequently for the Madonna and Magdalen photographs. In the later version of *Freshwater* the maid becomes Mary (Ryan), the servant and model who married a peer.

"A drawing room at Dimbola, hung with photographs" (page 55).

The Virginia Woolf–Desmond MacCarthy letter also speaks of plans to use masses of Cameron photographs, shawls, cameos, and other props appearing in the stage directions.

"She plucks at her wrist" (page 58).

"She plucks at her wrist" appears in Vanessa's notes for her part as Mrs. Cameron in the 1935 version. The appearance of the phrase here has led some to question whether this is in fact an earlier version. I suspect that Vanessa and Virginia were simply using both versions at the time of their 1935 production.

"I hate the dreadful hollow beneath the little wood" (page 58).

The line should read ". . . behind the little wood."

"Maud, Maud, Maud, they are crying and calling" (page 68).

In an amusing passage from "The Searchlight" manuscript the rooks are flying over Farringford crying "Maud, Maud, Maud."

"She is coming, my own, my dear" (page 69).

The line should read "She is coming, my own, my sweet."

"Middleton Murry and the *Adelphi*" (page 72).

These jibes at Murry, whose directorship of the *Adelphi* began in 1923 and who by 1935 was no longer part of Virginia's scene, are the sort of internal evidence that helps to identify this manuscript as the earlier version.